GREAT TASTES
DRINKS

First published in 2010 by Bay Books, an imprint of Murdoch Books Pty Limited
This edition published in 2010.

Murdoch Books Australia
Pier 8/9
23 Hickson Road
Millers Point NSW 2000
Phone: +61 (0) 2 8220 2000
Fax: +61 (0) 2 8220 2558
www.murdochbooks.com.au

Murdoch Books UK Limited
Erico House, 6th Floor
93–99 Upper Richmond Road
Putney, London SW15 2TG
Phone: +44 (0) 20 8785 5995
Fax: +44 (0) 20 8785 5985
www.murdochbooks.co.uk

Chief Executive: Juliet Rogers
Publishing Director: Kay Scarlett
Publisher: Lynn Lewis
Senior Designer: Heather Menzies
Design: Transformer Creative
Production: Kita George

ISBN: 9780681690820

PRINTED IN CHINA

OVEN GUIDE: You may find cooking times vary depending on the oven you are using. For fan-forced ovens, as a general rule, set the oven
temperature to 20°C (35°F) lower than indicated in the recipe.

GREAT TASTES
DRINKS

More than 120 easy recipes for every day

bay books

CONTENTS

DRINKS BASICS

Juices and smoothies, shakes, chocolate drinks, coffees and teas and a myriad of mocktails and cocktails can all easily be made at home. All require the use of good-quality ingredients and the help of the appropriate kitchen appliances. Many kitchens now have a juicer sitting on the bench for those early-morning wake-you-up drinks. And, increasingly, sophisticated coffee-making machines are finding their way into the family home. It's worth investing in the best appliances you can afford.

Juices and smoothies

Most juices and smoothies are made with one of two pieces of equipment — a juicer or a blender. Some recipes require both; others also involve the use of a citrus press. When choosing a juicer, prices and reliability go hand in hand upwards, but here are a few things to consider before you buy: Does the juicer have parts that are dishwasher proof? What is the motor's size? How easy will it be to clean? How wide is the chute (will it be able to cope with whole fruit and vegetables)? Does it have low and high speeds? Is there a slide-in froth separator (which is about as good as it gets)? The more expensive juicers generally do work better, and last longer. They also extract more juice per fruit so you get more for your money.

Juicers work by a process of centrifugal motion, spinning the fruit or vegetable pieces in a filter basket fitted with a rotating cutting disk, thus separating the juice from the pulp. The juice comes out the spout; the leftover pulp goes into a disposal container. A few things to remember: Always use the plunger to push food down the chute, not your fingers; use the plunger slowly (this will ensure the greatest amount of juice is extracted from the pulp, and will ease the strain on the filter basket and motor); and put the juice jug or a glass under the spout before turning on. If you wish, line the pulp-collecting container with a plastic bag, as that can be easily discarded later. Do not let the pulp-collecting container overfill.

Fruit and vegetables that have a high water content, such as tomatoes and watermelon, should be juiced on a slow speed (if your machine has this option); and hard ingredients such as carrots, apples, beetroot and fennel will break down best on a higher speed.

All juicers need cleaning. Sad but true. Always ensure that the stainless-steel filter is thoroughly clean before use. This means cleaning it properly immediately after each use. Once any pulp dries on the filter, it will clog the pores and is a chore to remove. Watch your fingers when cleaning the filter basket. Some juicers come with a special brush for washing the basket.

The best raw ingredients

Always use good-quality ingredients — there is nothing to mask their flavours, after all. Use organic where possible, and refrain from using ingredients until they are fully ripe. Use fruit and vegetables straight from the refrigerator, so that the end result is perfectly chilled. If you freeze fruit, such as berries, cherries, chopped mango and overripe banana, use the fruit within two weeks. After that, the flavour fades. Unless otherwise stated, juice fruit and vegetables with the skin on. Remove all pits and hard stones before using. The seeds can stay if juicing but remove if blending. When juicing fresh herbs or small quantities of ingredients such as a piece of ginger or alfalfa sprouts, bunch them together or send them through the juicer alternating with a main ingredient.

Wash produce before use, scrubbing tough-skinned varieties with a soft brush. Chop ingredients only when you are ready to put the pieces in the juicer or blender; otherwise, you will cause unnecessary vitamin loss.

Adjust the consistency of drinks by adding water or still mineral water for a thinner drink, or frozen fruit, crushed ice or frozen yoghurt for a thicker one. Sweeten juices by adding a dash of honey, maple syrup or some ripe banana (though this will affect the drink's consistency). If adding sugar, always use caster (superfine) sugar as it dissolves easily.

Whole ice cubes can be added to the blender, but crushing them first gives a better result. There is something therapeutic about smashing ice cubes wrapped in a tea towel (dish towel) against the kitchen bench or hitting them with a rolling pin. Finally, drink juices immediately. If you wait, ingredients will start separating, colours will change, nutritional values will begin to fade ... and the flavour goes all wrong. This is especially true of juices containing apple and pear, which oxidize quickly. .

Cocktails and mocktails

There's no special mystique involved in cocktail making. It is an easy art to master and with a little dedicated practice you'll be serving drinks with flair and panache. All you need are a few simple implements, some basic ingredients, a steady hand, a highly developed sense of fun and a rampant imagination.

Remember that although they may taste innocent, cocktails are highly intoxicating. So if you're hosting a cocktail party, offer plenty of food and non-alcoholic refreshments so your guests will remember what a fabulous time they had!

The bar essentials

One implement you'll definitely need to buy is a cocktail shaker, available in two basic types. A standard shaker usually has three stainless-steel pieces — a canister that holds the ice, a lid with an inbuilt strainer that seals tightly over the top, and a twist-off cap. The Boston shaker often has a mixing glass as its base, snugly overlapped by a stainless-steel top. It does not have an inbuilt strainer, so you'll need a separate strainer to filter the drink when pouring. The most widely used is a hawthorn strainer, which has a distinctive circular head with a spring coil that fits sweetly around the metal half of a Boston shaker.

The other major implement most budding cocktail stars will need is an electric blender. If you're a total fanatic, invest in a heavy-duty model with a powerful motor and sturdy blades that can cope with whole ice cubes (check the manufacturer's instructions). If your blender is a little lightweight, you'll need to crush the ice cubes before putting them in the blender. To help your blades last longer, add the liquid ingredients to the blender first, then the ice.

Next, find yourself a large jug with a pouring spout to use as a mixing glass; this is especially useful for making multiple quantities of mixed drinks. You'll also need measuring spoons and a jigger for measuring alcohol.).

A long-handled bar spoon (preferably stainless steel) is used for stirring cocktails and 'floating' ingredients in layered drinks.| It can also be used for 'muddling' fruit and herbs, or you could buy a special muddler, which is essentially a wooden pestle, from specialist kitchen stores.

Ice, ice and more ice is essential to a cool cocktail, so you'll need plenty of ice-cube trays, an ice bucket for storing ice cubes, and a pair of tongs or an ice scoop for dispensing ice.

Other must-haves include a citrus squeezer, a chopping board, a sharp fruit knife, a sharp vegetable peeler and a zester. For those finishing touches, stock up on plain and coloured toothpicks, pretty cocktail umbrellas, swizzle sticks and straws of many colours.

Glass class

Purists will insist on using the right glass for every drink. Short mixed drinks 'on the rocks' are served in an old-fashioned glass or tumbler; long mixed drinks are shaken, stirred or built in a highball glass or in a slightly deeper Collins glass. Cocktails without ice are poured into stemmed glasses to keep hot hands away from the drink. 'Short' drinks such as martinis are served in a triangular cocktail or martini glass. Champagne cocktails and some wine cocktails use a champagne flute, while cocktails containing egg yolks are usually dished out in goblets. Mixed or blended drinks are often served in a tulip-shaped glass. Other glasses include shot glasses, brandy balloons (glasses for swirling, sniffing and swilling fine brandies) and the sour glass, which resembles a champagne flute but has a shorter stem.

Tricks of the trade

Chill all your ingredients before using, and chill the glasses, too, or leave a scoop of ice in them while preparing your drinks. Always use fresh ice for each drink, and the best ingredients you can source. Have all ingredients ready to go before you start mixing, shaking, stirring or building your drinks, and don't overfill shakers or mixers. To avoid spillage, never fill a glass to the brim,

and remember to leave room for the garnish. Finally, make each drink to order, as cocktails lose their 'verve' over time.

Blending Purée the cocktail ingredients in a blender to a smooth, drinkable consistency, but don't overblend or you'll have a weak, watery concoction. Unless you have a heavy-duty blender, use crushed ice rather than ice cubes in your blender.

Shaking Half-fill the cocktail shaker with crushed ice, add the other ingredients and vertically shake the canister vigorously until the shaker is frosty outside (10 seconds should do, but if your cocktail is very creamy or syrupy you might need to double the time). Strain into a chilled glass. Carbonated drinks should never be shaken or they'll lose their fizz.

Stirring For sparkling clean looks, certain cocktails are stirred in a mixing glass or jug with a handful of ice cubes. This chills the alcohol quickly, without diluting it. The cocktail is then strained into a glass.

Floating Gently pour the liqueur or spirit into the glass over the back of a spoon. Add the ingredients in the order specified in the recipe and do not mix — you are creating a layered effect.

Muddling Grind, crush or mash fresh fruit or herbs with sugar (usually in a cocktail shaker) using a muddler or bar spoon to release all the flavours.

Snazzy ice cubes Freeze fruit juice in an ice-cube tray, perhaps with some mint leaves or diced fruit.

For a special touch

Many recipes call for sugar syrup, which you can buy or very easily make. Simply place equal quantities of water and sugar in a saucepan and stir well to dissolve the sugar. Bring to the boil, reduce the heat and simmer until reduced by half. Allow to cool, pour into an airtight container and refrigerate.

JUICES

PINEAPPLE KICK

MAKES 2 X 250 ML GLASSES

3 oranges, peeled

600 g (1 lb 5 oz) peeled and chopped fresh pineapple

3.5 cm (1½ inch) piece fresh ginger, peeled

1 **Cut the oranges** into pieces to fit the juicer.

2 **Using the plunger**, push the orange pieces, pineapple and ginger through the juicer and into a pitcher.

3 **Pour into glasses** and serve with ice.

MORNING BLENDED FRUIT JUICE

½ fresh pineapple, peeled and cored

375 ml (13 fl oz/1½ cups) fresh orange juice

1 large pear, cored, chopped

1 banana, chopped

40 g (1½ oz) chopped pawpaw

1 Chop the pineapple flesh into pieces and place in the blender. Add the orange juice, pear, banana and pawpaw and blend together until smooth. Serve at once.

WATERMELON BREAKFAST JUICE

MAKES 2 LARGE GLASSES

700 g (1 lb 9 oz/3½ cups) chopped watermelon

2 tablespoons lime juice

1–2 cm (½–¾ inch) piece peeled ginger, grated, to taste

2 tablespoons chopped mint

1 Blend the watermelon, lime juice, ginger and mint in a blender in short bursts. (Be careful not to overblend or the mixture will go frothy.)

THINK PINK

MAKES 2 LARGE GLASSES

3 pink grapefruit, peeled

250 g (9 oz) strawberries, hulled

375 ml (13 fl oz/1½ cups) guava juice

ice cubes, to serve

1 **Juice the grapefruit** and strawberries through a juice extractor. Stir through the guava juice and serve over ice.

WATERMELON, PINEAPPLE AND GINGER COOLER

SERVES 4

1 kg (2 lb 4 oz) seedless watermelon

4 cm (1½ in) piece young ginger

250 ml (9 fl oz/1 cup) pineapple juice, chilled

250 ml (9 fl oz/1 cup) tropical fruit juice, chilled

ice cubes, to serve

1 **Remove the skin** from the watermelon and cut the flesh into large chunks. Peel and finely grate the ginger.

2 **Put the watermelon and ginger** in a blender and whizz for 20–25 seconds, or until smooth. With the motor running, add the pineapple and tropical fruit juices and whizz until combined.

3 **Pour into four glasses** and top with ice cubes. Stir briskly and serve immediately.

Note: If preferred, the watermelon may be chilled after being skinned and cut into chunks. Any tropical juice such as guava, mango or mixed fruit can be used.

MANDARIN AND MANGO CHILL

MAKES 2 X 375 ML GLASSES

1 mango, cut into slices

500 ml (17 fl oz/2 cups) mandarin juice

125 ml (4 fl oz/½ cup) lime juice cordial

375 ml (13 fl oz/1½ cups) soda water

2 tablespoons caster (superfine) sugar

ice cubes

1 **Freeze the mango** for about 1 hour, or until semi-frozen.

2 **Combine the juice,** cordial, soda water and sugar in a pitcher.

3 **Place the mango slices** and some ice cubes into each glass, then pour in the juice mix.

RED GRAPE AND ROCKMELON JUICE

MAKES 2 MEDIUM GLASSES

500 g (1 lb 2 oz) red seedless grapes

1 rockmelon (or other orange-fleshed melon), peeled, seeded and chopped

2 cm (¾ in) piece ginger

1 **Juice the grapes,** rockmelon and ginger through a juice extractor. Stir to combine.

STRANGE BIRD

500 g (1 lb 2 oz) strawberries, hulled

6 kiwifruit, peeled

ice cubes, to serve

1 **Juice the strawberries** and kiwifruit through a juice extractor. Stir to combine and serve over ice.

GREEN PUNCH

MAKES 2 X 250 ML GLASSES

1 green apple, cored

½ medium honeydew melon, peeled, seeds removed

2 oranges, peeled

ice cubes, to serve

1 **Cut the apple,** melon and oranges into pieces to fit into the juicer.

2 **Using the plunger,** push all the ingredients through the juicer and into a jug.

3 **Pour into glasses** and serve with ice.

PEAR, APPLE AND GINGER JUICE

MAKES 2 X 375 ML GLASSES

2.5 cm (1 inch) piece fresh ginger, peeled

3 ripe pears, cored, quartered, chilled

5 granny smith apples, quartered, chilled

1 **Using a juicer,** juice the ginger, pear and apple together. Pour into jug.

2 **Combine well** and serve immediately.

Note: Ensure the fruit is well chilled before juicing as this drink should be served immediately—separation of flavours occurs quickly and the fruit will discolour.

FUZZY PEACH

MAKES 2 LARGE GLASSES

6 peaches, stones removed

1 lemon, peeled

large pinch freshly grated nutmeg

250 ml (9 fl oz/1 cup) dry ginger ale

ice cubes, to serve

1 **Juice the peaches** and lemon through a juice extractor. Stir through the nutmeg and dry ginger ale. Serve over ice.

2 **Add a little heat** to sun-warmed peaches with a pinch of freshly grated nutmeg.

PEAR, MELON AND PEPPERMINT JUICE

MAKES 4 SMALL GLASSES

3 pears, stalks removed

½ small rockmelon (or other orange-fleshed melon), peeled, seeded and chopped

few peppermint leaves

ice cubes, to serve

1 Juice the pears, rockmelon and peppermint leaves through a juice extractor. Stir to combine and serve over ice.

Notes: The best way to select a ripe melon is to use your nose — if it has a strong sweet fragrance and thick raised netting you can almost guarantee it is ready to eat.

Peppermint is well known as a stomach calmer and its fresh aroma can also lift your mood.

BLACKCURRANT CRUSH

MAKES 4 X 300 ML GLASSES

750 ml (27 fl oz/3 cups) apple and
   blackcurrant juice

500 ml (17 fl oz/2 cups) soda water
   (club soda)

1 tablespoon caster (superfine) sugar

150 g (6 oz) blueberries

ice cubes

1 **Place the apple and blackcurrant juice,** soda water,
sugar and blueberries into a blender and blend until smooth.

2 **Serve in chilled glasses** over ice.

Note: If you have a top-quality blender, you may wish to
add the ice cubes when blending the other ingredients to
make a slushy.

LEMON BARLEY WATER

MAKES 4 X 250 ML GLASSES

110 g (4 oz/½ cup) pearl barley

3 lemons

125 g (5 oz/½ cup) caster sugar

crushed ice

lemon slices

1 **Wash the barley well** and place in a medium pan. Using a sharp vegetable peeler, remove the peel from the lemons, avoiding the bitter white pith. Squeeze out the juice and set aside. Add peel and 1.75 litres (62 fl oz/7 cups) cold water to the barley; bring to the boil. Simmer briskly for 30 minutes. Add the sugar and mix to dissolve. Allow to cool.

2 **Strain the liquid into a jug** and add the lemon juice. Serve over crushed ice and garnish with lemon slices.

SWEET AND SPICY PLUM

MAKES 2 MEDIUM GLASSES

10 small plums, stones removed

2.5 cm (1 inch) piece ginger, peeled

200 g (7 oz) cherries, pitted

3 oranges, peeled

1 large handful mint leaves

1 teaspoon honey

ice cubes, to serve

1 Juice the plums, ginger, cherries, oranges and mint leaves through a juice extractor. Stir through the honey, mixing well, and serve over ice.

HONEYDEW, PINEAPPLE AND MINT JUICE

MAKES 2 LARGE GLASSES

1 honeydew melon, peeled, seeded and chopped

1 small pineapple, peeled

1 medium handful mint leaves

1 **Juice the honeydew,** pineapple and mint leaves through a juice extractor. Stir to combine.

MANGO SUMMER HAZE

MAKES 6 LARGE GLASSES

2 mangoes, peeled and chopped

500 ml (17 fl oz/2 cups) orange juice

55 g (2 oz.¼ cup) caster (superfine) sugar

500 ml (17 fl oz/2 cups) sparkling mineral water

ice cubes, to serve

mango slices, to garnish, optional

1 **Blend the mango,** orange juice and sugar in a blender until smooth. Stir through the mineral water. Serve over ice and garnish with fresh mango slices, if desired.

KIWI DELIGHT

MAKES 4 SMALL GLASSES

3 kiwifruit, peeled and sliced

80 g (3 oz/½ cup) peeld and chopped fresh pineapple

1 banana, chopped

250 ml (9 fl oz/1 cup) tropical fruit juice

2 ice cubes

1 **Blend the kiwifruit,** pineapple, banana, fruit juice and ice cubes in a blender until smooth.

PASSIONFRUIT SYRUP

MAKES 375 ML (1½ CUPS)

6 panama or large passionfruit

125 ml (4 fl oz/½ cup) lemon juice

115 g (4 oz/½ cup) caster (superfine) sugar

1 Combine the passionfruit pulp, lemon juice, sugar and 500 ml (17 fl oz/2 cups) water in a saucepan over high heat. Stir until the sugar has dissolved. Bring to the boil, reduce to a simmer and cook for 1½ hours or until reduced by half and slightly syrupy. Allow to cool, then strain, pressing on the solids. Pour into a very clean glass jar or bottle and seal. Refrigerate for up to 2 weeks.

Note: To serve, pour a little syrup into a glass with ice and top with soda water, lemonade or dry ginger ale.

LEMON SOOTHER

MAKES 4 MEDIUM GLASSES

½ lemon, thinly sliced

1 large lemon thyme sprig

1 stem lemon grass, bruised

honey, to taste, optional

1   Put the lemon, lemon thyme and lemon grass in the base of a large heatproof pitcher and pour in 1 litre (35 fl oz/4 cups) boiling water. Set aside to infuse for 10–15 minutes. Serve hot or warm with some honey, if desired.

PINE LIME AND STRAWBERRY BURST

MAKES 2 MEDIUM GLASSES

1 pineapple, peeled

2 limes, peeled

500 g (1 lb 2 oz) strawberries, hulled

1 **Juice the pineapple,** limes and strawberries through a juice extractor. Stir to combine.

ORANGE CITRUS CRUSH

MAKES 4 MEDIUM GLASSES

12 navel oranges

zest and juice of 1 lime

sugar, to taste

ice cubes, to serve

1 Segment two of the oranges and juice the remainder in a citrus press — don't strain the juice, you can keep the pulp in it. Add the lime zest and juice to the orange juice. Add the orange segments and sugar. Stir to combine. Serve over ice.

Note: The juice of navel oranges will turn bitter within a few minutes of juicing, so drink this juice immediately. Use blood oranges when they're in season.

RED GINGER

MAKES 4 SHOT GLASSES

500 g (1 lb 2 oz) red seedless grapes

10 small plums, stones removed

2 limes, peeled

2.5 cm (1 inch) piece ginger, peeled

1 medium handful mint leaves

ice cubes, to serve

1 **Juice the grapes,** plums, limes, ginger and mint through a juice extractor. Stir to combine and serve over ice.

VANILLA AND APRICOT ORANGE INFUSION

MAKES 6 MEDIUM GLASSES

200 g (7 oz) dried apricots, chopped

1 vanilla bean, chopped

zest of 1 orange

55 g (2 oz/¼ cup) caster (superfine) sugar

small pinch cloves, optional

ice cubes, to serve

1 Combine the apricots, vanilla bean, orange zest, sugar, cloves and 3 litres (105 fl oz/12 cups) water in a large saucepan. Stir over high heat until the sugar has dissolved. Bring to the boil, then reduce the heat and gently simmer for 20 minutes. Set aside to cool. Strain and chill well. Stir to combine and serve over ice.

GREEN APPLE AND LEMON THIRST QUENCHER

MAKES 2 X 350 ML GLASSES

80 ml (3 fl oz/⅓ cup) lemon juice, chilled

6 medium (1 kg/2 lb 4 oz) green apples, chilled

mint leaves, to garnish

1 Pour the lemon juice into a jug.

2 Wash the apples and cut into smaller pieces to fit into the juicer. Using the plunger, push the apples through the juicer.

3 Add the apple juice to the lemon juice and stir well. Garnish with mint leaves and serve immediately.

Note: This is a refreshing, slightly tart drink. If the apples and lemons are not cold, throw a handful of ice cubes into the blender and pulse.

FENNEL AND ORANGE JUICE

MAKES 2 X 375 ML GLASSES

8 oranges
150 g (6 oz) baby fennel

1 **Peel and quarter the oranges,** and remove any seeds. Trim the fennel and cut in half.

2 **Using a juicer,** push the fennel through first to release the flavours, then juice the orange. Chill well.

3 **Combine well** before serving.

Note: When in season, the flavour will be stronger in larger, more developed fennel.

SPRING CLEAN YOUR BODY

MAKES 4 X 250 ML GLASSES

2 large cucumbers

6 medium (600 g/2 oz) carrots

1 large green apple

2 celery stalks, including leaves

1 large beetroot (beet)

1 **Remove the skin from the cucumbers.** Cut the cucumbers, carrots, apple and celery into pieces to fit the juicer.

2 **Scrub the beetroot** with a firm brush to remove any dirt and cut to fit the juicer.

3 **Using the plunger,** push the fruit and vegetables through the juicer into a large pitcher.

4 **Serve chilled** or with ice.

DINNER IN A GLASS

MAKES 2 X 400 ML GLASSES

10–12 medium carrots

1 medium beetroot (beet)

2 medium green apples

2 English spinach leaves

2 celery stalks

1 **Cut the carrots** to fit the juicer.

2 **Scrub the beetroot** to ensure all the dirt is removed. Cut the beetroot and apples to fit the juicer.

3 **Using the plunger,** push all the ingredients through the juicer and into a large pitcer.

4 **Serve chilled** or over ice.

VEGETABLE JUICE

SERVES 2

1 beetroot (beet), scrubbed

10–12 carrots

2 green apples, stalks removed

2 large English spinach leaves

2 celery stalks

1 **Wash the vegetables** and cut them into pieces so they will fit into your juice extractor. Juice the beetroot, carrots, apples, spinach and celery in the juice extractor.

2 **Return some of the pulp** left in the extractor to the juice (the pulp contains lots of fibre). Stir well to combine and serve well chilled.

BEETROOT, CARROT AND GINGER JUICE

MAKES 2 SMALL GLASSES

1 beetroot (beet), scrubbed

6 carrots

2.5 cm (1 inch) piece ginger, peeled

1 **Juice the beetroot**, carrots and ginger through a juice extractor. Stir to combine.

HONEYED CARROTS

MAKES 2 MEDIUM GLASSES

1 kg (2 lb 4 oz) carrots

125 g (5 oz) alfalfa sprouts

4 pears, stalks removed

1–2 teaspoons honey, to taste

carrot strips, for garnish (optional)

1 **Juice the carrots,** alfalfa and pears through a juice extractor. Stir through the honey. Garnish with carrot strips, if desired.

COOL AS A CUCUMBER

MAKES 2 LARGE GLASSES

3 large cucumbers

3 limes, peeled

1 large handful mint leaves

1½ tablespoons caster (superfine) sugar

1 **Juice the cucumbers,** limes and mint through a juice
extractor. Stir through the sugar.

SPINACH ENERGIZER

MAKES 2 LARGE GLASSES

50 g (2 oz/2 cups) baby English spinach
    leaves

1 large cucumber

3 apples, stalks removed

3 celery stalks

1 baby fennel

1 large handful parsley

1 **Juice the spinach,** cucumber, apples, celery, fennel and
parsley through a juice extractor. Stir to combine.

CELERY, TOMATO AND PARSLEY JUICE

MAKES 2 X 400 ML GLASSES

1 large handful fresh parsley

6 vine-ripened tomatoes, quartered

4 celery stalks, trimmed

1 **Using a juicer,** push through the parsley leaves to infuse the flavour. Then juice the tomatoes and celery. Chill well.

2 **Before serving,** mix together well and garnish with a stick of celery as a swizzle stick.

Note: For extra spice, add a few drops of Tabasco and freshly ground black pepper.

SMOOTHIES & SHAKES

CHOCOLATE CARAMEL THICK SHAKE

SERVES 4

2 x 60 g (2¼ oz) caramel chocolate bars, roughly chopped (see Note)

750 ml (26 fl oz/3 cups) chocolate ice cream

375 ml (13 fl oz/1½ cups) milk

2 tablespoons drinking chocolate powder

1 Put the caramel bars and ice cream in a blender and whizz for 30 seconds, or until the bars are finely chopped.

2 Add the milk and drinking chocolate powder and blend until thick and frothy. There will be some pieces of caramel bar left in the bottom of the blender.

3 Pour into four glasses. Spoon out the remaining pieces of caramel bar and divide among the glasses.

Note: A caramel chocolate bar such as a Mars Bar or Moro is perfect for this recipe. Or, try using your favourite caramel chocolate bar.

DOUBLE STRAWBERRY THICK SHAKE

SERVES 4

250 g (9 oz/1⅔ cups) strawberries

4 scoops strawberry ice cream

2 tablespoons malted milk powder

375 ml (13 fl oz/1½ cups) milk

extra malted milk powder, to serve

1 Select two small strawberries for garnishing and halve them from top to bottom, cutting through the hull. Without slicing all the way through, cut each half from bottom to top into two slices joined at the stalk. Gently fan out the slices.

2 Hull the remaining strawberries and cut them in half, removing the white core if it is very noticeable. Place the strawberries, ice cream and malted milk powder in a blender and whizz for 20–25 seconds, or until thick and smooth.

3 Add the milk and whizz for 25–30 seconds, or until frothy. Pour into four glasses and top each with one of the reserved fanned strawberry halves. Sprinkle with the extra malted milk powder. Serve immediately.

ENERGY FRUIT SMOOTHIE

SERVES 4

½ (about 650 g/1 lb 7 oz) rockmelon or any orange-fleshed melon

1 mango

2 tablespoons toasted muesli

1 tablespoon honey

1 tablespoon malted milk powder

100 g (4 oz/⅓ cup) Greek-style apricot yoghurt

125 ml (4 fl oz/½ cup) orange juice

250 ml (9 fl oz/1 cup) skim milk

1 Peel the melon, scoop out the seeds and roughly chop the flesh. Prepare the mango by slicing off the cheeks with a sharp knife. Using a large spoon, scoop the flesh out of the skin. Cut the flesh into chunks.

2 Put the melon, mango and toasted muesli in a blender and whizz for 20 seconds, or until smooth. Add the honey, malted milk powder and yoghurt and whizz for 10 seconds. Add orange juice and skim milk and whizz for 30 seconds, or until foaming. Pour into four glasses to serve.

Note: The fruit may be chilled beforehand for a colder drink. Alternatively, the smoothie can be chilled for up to 2 hours before serving.

BANANA SMOOTHIE

SERVES 2

2 just-ripe bananas

60 g (2 oz/¼ cup) low-fat vanilla or
   fruit-flavoured yoghurt

500 ml (17 fl oz/2 cups) low-fat milk

2 tbsp wheat germ or oat bran

freshly grated nutmeg, to taste

1 Put the bananas in a blender or food processor. Add the yoghurt, milk, wheat germ and nutmeg. Blend or process until smooth, then pour into two chilled glasses.

Note: Use other fruit in place of the bananas, such as berries, pears, apricots, plums, peaches or nectarines. Select the best of the season.

VERY BERRY

MAKES 4 SMALL GLASSES

50 g (2 oz/1 cup) low-fat strawberry
   yoghurt

125 ml (4 fl oz/½ cup) cranberry juice,
   chilled

250 g (9 oz) strawberries, hulled and
   quartered

125 g (4 oz) frozen raspberries

1 Combine the yoghurt and cranberry juice in a blender. Add quartered strawberries and 80 g (3 oz) of the raspberries. Blend until smooth.

2 Pour into chilled glasses and top with the remaining frozen raspberries. Serve with a spoon as it is quite thick.

GREAT TASTES DRINKS

SUMMER STRAWBERRY SMOOTHIE

1 tablespoon strawberry flavouring

250 ml (9 fl oz/1 cup) wildberry drinking
  yoghurt

250 g (9 oz) strawberries, hulled

4 scoops frozen strawberry yoghurt

few drops vanilla essence

ice cubes

1 Combine the strawberry flavouring, drinking yoghurt, strawberries, frozen yoghurt and vanilla in a blender and process until smooth.

2 Pour over plenty of ice to serve.

APPLE AND BLACKCURRANT SHAKE

MAKES 2 MEDIUM GLASSES

250 ml (9 fl oz/1 cup) apple and
    blackcurrant juice

2 tablespoons natural yoghurt

185 ml (6 fl oz/¾ cup) milk

3 scoops vanilla ice cream

1 **Blend the juice,** yoghurt, milk and ice cream in a blender
until well combined and fluffy.

MAKES 4 SMALL GLASSES

2 bananas, chopped

1 large mango, peeled and chopped

500 ml (17 fl oz/2 cups) skim milk

500 ml (17 fl oz/2 cups) orange juice or
    pink grapefruit juice

1 **Blend the banana,** mango, milk and orange or pink
grapefruit juice in a blender until smooth. Pour into a jug
and chill.

APRICOT SMOOTHIE

SERVES 4

500 ml (17 fl oz/2 cups) milk

420 g (15 oz) tin apricots in light syrup

200 g (7 oz/¾ cup) apricot yoghurt

1 tablespoon wheat germ or lecithin meal

½ teaspoon ground cinnamon

honey, optional, to taste

extra ground cinnamon, to serve

1 Put the milk in a covered container in the freezer for 30 minutes to make it very cold. It should be cold but not icy.

2 Drain the apricots, then put them in a blender. Add the milk, yoghurt, wheat germ or lecithin meal, and cinnamon. Whizz for 30 seconds, or until smooth. Sweeten with honey, to taste, if using.

3 Pour into four glasses and sprinkle with a little extra cinnamon. Serve immediately.

Notes: Low-fat milk and yoghurt can be used, if preferred. For a more refreshing smoothie, chill the apricots before use.

SUMMER FRUIT SOY SMOOTHIE

1 banana

4 peaches, chopped

175 g (6 oz/¾ cup) apricot and mango soy yoghurt or vanilla soy yoghurt

1 tablespoon lecithin meal, from health food stores

1 teaspoon natural vanilla extract

625 ml (22 fl oz/2½ cups) plain soy milk or vanilla soy milk

1 tablespoon maple syrup, optional

extra peach slices, to serve

ice cubes, to serve

1 **Put the banana**, peach, yoghurt, lecithin meal, vanilla extract and 250 ml (9 fl oz/1 cup) of the soy milk in a blender. Whizz for 30 seconds, or until smooth.

2 **Add the remaining soy milk** and whizz for a further 30 seconds, or until combined. Taste for sweetness and add the maple syrup, if using. Put the ice and extra peach slices in four glasses, pour in the smoothie and serve immediately.

Notes: Use fat-free soy milk and yoghurt if preferred. If fresh peaches are not available, use 4 tinned peach halves.

WATERMELON SMOOTHIE

MAKES 4 SMALL GLASSES

600 g (1 lb 6 oz/3 cups) chopped
    watermelon (see Note)

125 g (5 oz/½ cup) yoghurt

250 ml (9 fl oz/1 cup) milk

1 tablespoon caster (superfine) sugar

2 scoops vanilla ice cream

1 **Blend the watermelon,** yoghurt, milk and sugar in a
blender until smooth. Add ice cream and blend for a few
seconds, or until frothy.

Note: Use seedless watermelon if possible. Otherwise, pick
out as many seeds as you can before blending.

PAPAYA AND ORANGE SMOOTHIE

SERVES 2

1 medium (650 g/1 lb 7 oz) papaya
1 medium orange
6–8 ice cubes
200 g (7 oz) plain yoghurt
1–2 tablespoons caster (superfine) sugar
ground nutmeg, to garnish

1 **Peel the papaya** and remove the seeds. Cut the flesh into cubes. Peel the orange and roughly chop the flesh.

2 **Place the papaya,** orange and ice in a blender and blend until smooth. Blend in the yoghurt, and add sugar, to taste.

3 **Divide between two glasses,** sprinkle lightly with nutmeg and serve.

Note: This keeps well for 6 hours in the refrigerator and is best in both flavour and colour when the small Fijian papaya are used. Peach or apricot flavoured yoghurt may be used for added flavour.

PASSIONFRUIT AND VANILLA ICE CREAM WHIP

SERVES 2

4 passionfruit

100 g (4 oz) passionfruit yoghurt

500 ml (17 fl oz/2 cups) milk

1 tablespoon caster sugar

2 scoops vanilla ice cream

1 **Scoop out the pulp** from passionfruit and push through a sieve to remove the seeds. Place in the blender with the yoghurt, milk, sugar and ice cream and blend until smooth.

2 **Pour into tall glasses** and serve with an extra scoop of ice cream, if desired.

MELON SHAKE

SERVES 2

500 g (1 lb 2 oz) rockmelon, peeled and seeded

2 tablespoons honey

375 ml (13 fl oz/1½ cups) milk

5 scoops vanilla ice cream

ground nutmeg

1 Cut the rockmelon into 2.5 cm (1 inch) pieces and place in a blender. Mix for 30 seconds, or until smooth.

2 Add the honey, milk and ice cream and blend the mixture for a further 10–20 seconds, or until well combined and smooth. Serve sprinkled with nutmeg.

CREAMY RICH BANANA AND MACADAMIA SMOOTHIE

MAKES 2 LARGE GLASSES

2 very ripe bananas, slightly frozen (see Note)

100 g (4 oz) honey-roasted macadamias

2 tablespoons vanilla honey yoghurt

500 ml (17 fl oz/2 cups) milk

2 tablespoons wheat germ

1 banana, extra, halved lengthways

1 **Blend the frozen bananas,** 60 g (2 oz) of the macadamias, the yoghurt, milk and wheat germ in a blender for several minutes until thick and creamy. Finely chop the remaining macadamias and put on a plate. Toss the banana halves in the nuts to coat. Stand a banana half in each glass or stand on the glass edge. Pour in the smoothie.

Note: The bananas need to be very ripe. Peel and chop them, toss in lemon juice and freeze in an airtight container ready for use later on.

AVOCADO SMOOTHIE

MAKES 2 MEDIUM GLASSES

1 small avocado, peeled, stone removed

500 ml (17 fl oz/2 cups) milk

3 teaspoons honey

½ teaspoon natural vanilla extract (essence)

1 **Blend the avocado,** milk, honey and vanilla in a blender until smooth. Serve at once.

TROPICAL FRUIT SHAKE

SERVES 4

185 ml (6 fl oz/¾ cup) guava nectar or guava juice

2 tablespoons lemon juice

1 medium yellow papaya, about 650 g (1 lb 7 oz)

310 ml (11 fl oz/1¼ cups) pineapple juice

100 ml (4 fl oz) milk

2 small scoops vanilla ice cream

1–2 tablespoons honey, to taste

1 Combine the guava nectar or juice and lemon juice. Pour into ice cube trays and freeze until firm.

2 Peel the papaya and cut it into small cubes. Put papaya in a blender with the pineapple juice, milk and ice cream and whizz for 25 seconds, or until smooth. Add honey, to taste, and blend for 15–20 seconds, or until frothy.

3 Pour the shake into four glasses and divide the guava ice cubes among the glasses.

Note: For a more refreshing shake, chill the papaya before use.

BERRY WHIZZ

SERVES 4

250 g (9 oz/1⅔ cups) strawberries,
   hulled and chopped

150 g (6oz/1 cup) fresh or frozen
   blueberries (see Note)

185 g (72 oz/1½ cups) fresh or frozen
   raspberries

625 ml (22 fl oz/2½ cups) freshly
   squeezed orange juice

ice cubes

1–2 tablespoons caster (superfine) sugar,
   to taste

mint leaves, to serve

1 **Put the strawberries,** blueberries and raspberries in a blender with 250 ml (9 fl oz/1 cup) of the orange juice. Whizz for 35–45 seconds, or until smooth.

2 **Use a large spoon** to push the berry mixture through a sieve, discarding the solids.

3 **Crush the ice** in the blender (use the ice crusher button if the blender has one). Add sieved berry purée, the remaining orange juice and the sugar, to taste. Whizz to combine, then taste for sweetness, adding more sugar if necessary.

4 **Pour into four glasses** and top each with a sprig of mint. Serve immediately.

Note: Use 12 or more ice cubes if using fresh berries. If using frozen berries, you may prefer not to use ice cubes.

PLUM AND PRUNE TANG

SERVES 4

250 g (9 fl oz/1 cup) low-fat vanilla
   yoghurt

125 ml (4 fl oz/½ cup) buttermilk

315 ml (11 fl oz/1¼ cups) milk

150 g (5½ oz/1 cup) prunes, pitted and
   diced

200 g (7 oz/½ cup) diced fresh plums

8 large ice cubes

1 **Place the yoghurt**, buttermilk, milk, prunes, plums
and ice cubes in a blender. Blend until the mixture is
smooth and the ice cubes have been well incorporated.
Serve immediately.

BLUE MAPLE

SERVES 2

200 g (7 oz/1 cup) low-fat blueberry
   fromage frais or other low-fat fresh
   soft curd cheese such as quark

185 ml (6 fl oz/¾ cup) low-fat milk

1 tablespoon maple syrup

½ teaspoon ground cinnamon

300 g (11 oz) frozen blueberries

1   Blend the fromage frais, milk, maple syrup, cinnamon
and 250 g (9 oz) of the frozen blueberries in a blender until
smooth. Serve topped with the remaining blueberries.

CHOCOHOLIC THICK SHAKE

MAKES 2 MEDIUM GLASSES

125 ml (4 fl oz/½ cup) cold milk

50 g (2 oz) dark chocolate, grated

2 tablespoons chocolate syrup

2 tablespoons cream

4 scoops chocolate ice cream

2 scoops chocolate ice cream, extra

grated dark chocolate, to garnish

1 Blend the milk, chocolate, syrup, cream and ice cream in a blender until smooth.

2 Pour into chilled glasses. Top each glass with a scoop of ice cream and sprinkle with grated chocolate.

ICED CHOCOLATE

MAKES 1 MEDIUM GLASS

2 tablespoons rich chocolate topping

375 ml (13 fl oz/1½ cups) icy-cold milk

1 scoop vanilla ice cream

whipped cream

drinking chocolate

1 Pour the chocolate topping into a glass and swirl it around the sides.

2 Fill with the cold milk and add the ice cream.

3 Serve with a big swirl of whipped cream and dust with drinking chocolate.

APRICOT CRUMBLE SMOOTHIE

MAKES 2 LARGE GLASSES.

200 g (7 oz) tinned apricots in natural juice

200 g (7 oz) vanilla yoghurt

250 ml (9 fl oz/1 cup) milk

1 tablespoon wheat germ

1 tablespoon malted milk powder

large pinch ground cinnamon

1 **Blend the undrained apricots**, yoghurt, milk, wheat germ, malted milk powder and cinnamon in a blender until smooth.

Note: Tinned peaches, apples or pears can be used instead of the apricots.

ALMOND CHERRY SMOOTHIE

MAKES 2 LARGE GLASSES

375 ml (13 fl oz/1½ cups) almond milk

400 g (14 oz) cherries, pitted

¼ teaspoon natural vanilla extract (essence)

pinch ground cinnamon

4 large ice cubes

1 **Blend the almond milk,** cherries, vanilla, cinnamon and ice cubes in a blender until smooth.

Note: If you like a strong almond or marzipan flavour, add a dash of almond extract (essence).

COCONUT AND LYCHEE LASSI

SERVES 4

565 g (1 lb 4 oz) tin lychees in syrup

270 ml (10 fl oz) coconut milk

115 g (4 oz/½ cup) caster (superfine) sugar

1 lemon grass stem, white part only, bruised

grated zest and juice of 1 lime

200 g (7 oz/¾ cup) plain yoghurt

1 teaspoon dried basil seeds, optional (see Note)

lime wedges, to serve

1 **Drain the lychees,** reserving 150 ml (5 fl oz) of the syrup as well as the lychees. Put the syrup in a saucepan and add the coconut milk, sugar, lemon grass and lime zest. Stir over medium heat until the sugar has dissolved. Bring to the boil, then reduce the heat and simmer for 1 minute. Remove from the heat and set aside to infuse for 15 minutes.

2 **Strain the mixture** into a blender and add the reserved lychees and yoghurt. Whizz for 30 seconds, or until smooth. Add the lime juice and whizz until just combined. Refrigerate until very cold.

3 **When ready to serve,** put the basil seeds, if using, in a small bowl and cover with water. Set aside for 3–4 minutes, or until the seeds have swelled. Stir the lassi, then pour into four glasses and top with basil seeds. Serve with lime wedges.

Note: Dried basil seeds are available from Asian supermarkets. When soaked in water they swell and become gelatinous. They add texture to the drink but no discernible flavour.

MANGO LASSI

2 large mangoes, about 400 g (14 oz) each

500 g (1 lb 2 oz/2 cups) thick or Greek-style yoghurt

2 teaspoons lemon juice

3–4 tablespoons caster (superfine) sugar, to taste

ice cubes, optional, to serve

extra diced mango, to serve

1 Prepare the mangoes by slicing off the cheeks with a sharp knife. Using a large spoon, scoop the flesh out of the skin. Cut the flesh into chunks and put it in a blender with the yoghurt, lemon juice and 3 tablespoons of the sugar.

2 Add 185 ml (6 fl oz/¾ cup) of cold water and whizz for 40–60 seconds, or until smooth. Taste for sweetness and add extra sugar, if desired.

3 Put some ice cubes, if using, in the bottom of four glasses. Pour the lassi over the top and serve immediately, topped with diced mango.

COCONUT CREAM AND RASPBERRY SHAKE

MAKES 4 SMALL GLASSES

300 g (11 oz) raspberries

250 ml (9 fl oz/1 cup) apple and blackcurrant juice

400 ml (14 fl oz) coconut cream

2 scoops vanilla soy ice cream

marshmallows, to serve

1 Blend raspberries, apple and blackcurrant juice, coconut cream and ice cream in a blender for several minutes until thick and creamy. Thread marshmallows onto 4 swizzle sticks and serve with the shakes. Provide a straw and a long spoon with each glass.

Note: For a low-fat drink, blend the raspberries and juice with ice instead of coconut cream and ice cream.

CAROB PEANUT SMOOTHIE

MAKES 2 MEDIUM OR 4 SMALL
GLASSES

400 ml (14 oz) carob- or chocolate-
flavoured soy milk

2 very ripe bananas, chopped (see Note)

150 g (6 oz) silken tofu

2 tablespoons honey

1 tablespoon peanut butter

1 **Blend the soy milk,** banana, tofu, honey and peanut butter in a blender until smooth.

Note: Don't throw away bananas with blackened, spotted skin; their lush ripeness is the highlight of this smoothie.

CINNAMON AND CUSTARD SHAKE

SERVES 2

375 ml (13 fl oz/1½ cups) milk

185 ml (6 fl oz/¾ cup) prepared custard

3 teaspoons honey

1½ teaspoons ground cinnamon

3 scoops vanilla ice cream

ground cinnamon

1 **Blend the milk,** custard, honey, cinnamon and ice cream until smooth and fluffy.

2 **Pour the shake into tall glasses,** sprinkle with the extra cinnamon and serve immediately.

CHOC CHERRY SMOOTHIE

SERVES 2

500 ml (17 fl oz/2 cups) milk

55 g (2 oz/¼ cup) whole red glacé cherries

25 g (1 oz/¼ cup) desiccated coconut

1 tablespoon chocolate topping

3 scoops chocolate ice cream

1 Blend the milk, cherries, coconut, topping and ice cream until smooth and fluffy.

2 Pour into tall glasses and serve immediately.

STRAWBERRY LASSI

MAKES 2 SMALL GLASSES

250 g (9 oz) strawberries, hulled

300 g (11 oz) strawberry soy yoghurt

2 tablespoons honey

4 ice cubes

1 **Blend the strawberries,** yoghurt, honey, ice cubes and 2–3 tablespoons water in a blender until smooth. Garnish with any leftover strawberries.

BLUEBERRY STARTER

MAKES 2 X 375 ML GLASSES

200 g (7 oz) fresh or frozen blueberries

250 g (9 oz/1 cup) plain yoghurt

250 ml (9 fl oz/1 cup) milk

1 tablespoon wheat germ

1–2 teaspoons honey, or to taste

1 Blend the blueberries, yoghurt, milk, wheat germ and honey until smooth.

2 Pour into glasses and serve immediately.

Note: Frozen blueberries are perfect for this drink, allowing you to make it at any time of the year. There's no need to thaw the berries; just throw them into the blender straight from the freezer.

ALMOND AND NECTARINE MILK

SERVES 4

125 g (5 oz/¾ cup) blanched almonds

6 nectarines, peeled and chopped

115 g (4 oz/½ cup) caster (superfine) sugar

½ teaspoon lemon juice

grated nutmeg, to serve

1 Put the almonds in a bowl and cover with plenty of cold water. Soak overnight. Drain, then rinse and discard any nuts with blemishes.

2 Put the almonds in a blender or small processor fitted with the metal blade, add 150 ml (5 fl oz) of cold water and whizz for 25 seconds, or until smooth. Add another 250 ml (9 fl oz/1 cup) of cold water and whizz for 30–35 seconds. Set aside for 2 hours.

3 Strain the almond mixture into a bowl through muslin or a fine sieve, squeezing to extract the liquid. Discard the solids.

4 Wipe out the blender or processor with paper towels and add the nectarines and sugar. Whizz for 20 seconds, or until smooth, then add the almond milk and lemon juice. With the motor running, gradually pour in 125 ml (4 fl oz/½ cup) of cold water; chill.

5 When ready to serve, pour into four glasses and dust with nutmeg.

RASPBERRY AND BANANA LOW-FAT SMOOTHIE

SERVES 4

625 ml (22 fl oz/2½ cups) low-fat milk

2 bananas

125 g (5 oz/1 cup) fresh or frozen raspberries

200 g (7 oz/¾ cup) low-fat vanilla yoghurt

1 tablespoon oat bran or lecithin meal

1 **Put the milk in a covered container** in the freezer for 30 minutes to make it very cold. It should be cold but not icy.

2 **Peel and chop the bananas** and put them in a blender. Add the raspberries, yoghurt, oat bran or lecithin meal, and 250 ml (9 fl oz/1 cup) of the milk. Whizz for 30 seconds, or until smooth.

3 **Add remaining milk** and whizz for a further 30 seconds, or until combined. Pour into four glasses and serve immediately.

Note: Add 1 tablespoon of honey for sweetness, if desired.

SPORTS SHAKE

SERVES 2

500 ml (17 fl oz/2 cups) milk, chilled

2 tablespoons honey

2 eggs

½ teaspoon natural vanilla extract (essence)

1 tablespoon wheat germ

1 medium banana, sliced

1 Blend the milk, honey, eggs, vanilla, wheat germ and banana until smooth.

2 Chill well and serve.

BANANA SOY LATTE

MAKES 4 SMALL GLASSES

440 ml (15 fl oz/1¾ cups)
  coffee-flavoured soy milk

2 bananas, chopped

8 large ice cubes

1 teaspoon drinking chocolate

¼ teaspoon ground cinnamon

1 **Blend the soy milk** and banana in a blender until smooth. With the blender running, add the ice cubes one at a time until well incorporated. Serve sprinkled with the drinking chocolate and ground cinnamon.

COCONUT AND PASSIONFRUIT SMOOTHIE

MAKES 2 MEDIUM GLASSES

140 ml (5 fl oz) coconut milk

250 ml (9 fl oz/1 cup) milk

25 g (1 oz/¼ cup) desiccated coconut

¼ teaspoon natural vanilla extract (essence)

3 scoops vanilla ice cream

170 g (6 oz) tin passionfruit pulp in syrup

1 **Blend the coconut milk,** milk, coconut, vanilla, ice cream and half the passionfruit pulp until the mixture is smooth and has become fluffy.

2 **Stir in the remaining pulp** and serve immediately.

BREAKFAST SHAKE

MAKES 2 MEDIUM GLASSES

150 g (6 oz) fruit (passionfruit, mango, banana, peaches, strawberries, blueberries)

250 ml (9 fl oz/1 cup) milk

2 teaspoons wheat germ

1 tablespoon honey

60 g (2 oz/¼ cup) vanilla yoghurt

1 egg, optional

1 tablespoon malt powder

1 **Blend all the ingredients** in a blender for 30–60 seconds, or until well combined.

2 **Pour into chilled glasses** and serve immediately.

CHOCOLATE, COFFEE & TEA

THE ULTIMATE HOT CHOCOLATE

SERVES 2

60 g (2 oz) chopped good-quality dark
   chocolate

500 ml (17 fl oz/2 cups) milk, warmed

marshmallows, to serve

1 Put the chocolate in a saucepan. Add 2 tablespoons water and stir over low heat until the chocolate has melted.

2 Gradually pour in the milk, whisking until smooth and slightly frothy. Heat without boiling.

3 Pour into mugs and float one or two marshmallows on top.

RICH MOCHA WARMER

SERVES 4

200 ml (7 fl oz) freshly brewed strong espresso coffee

50 g (2 oz/⅓ cup) roughly chopped good-quality dark chocolate

500 ml (17 fl oz/2 cups) milk

raw or golden caster (superfine) sugar, to taste

whipped cream, to serve

4 cinnamon sticks, to serve (optional)

chocolate-coated coffee beans, to serve (optional)

grated nutmeg, to serve

1 Put the hot coffee and chocolate in a 1 litre (35 fl oz/ 4 cup) heatproof jug and set aside for 1–1½ minutes until the chocolate has melted, stirring once or twice.

2 Meanwhile, put the milk in a small saucepan and gently warm over low heat to just below boiling point. Pour the milk into the jug containing the coffee mixture. Using an immersion blender fitted with a blending or general purpose blade, whizz for 30–45 seconds, or until smooth and frothy. Add the sugar, to taste.

3 Pour into four warmed mugs or latte glasses and top each drink with a scoop of whipped cream. Add cinnamon sticks and chocolate-coated coffee beans, if using. Sprinkle with nutmeg and serve immediately.

SPANISH HOT CHOCOLATE

SERVES 4

500 ml (17 fl oz/2 cups) milk

4 cm x 3 cm (1½ x 1¼ in) piece orange zest, white pith removed, lightly scored

250 g (9 oz/1⅔ cups) finely chopped good-quality dark chocolate

1 Put the milk and orange zest in a heavy-based saucepan. Bring to the boil over medium heat; stir constantly. As soon as the milk comes to the boil, remove the pan from the heat and set aside to for 5 minutes to allow the flavour to develop.

2 Discard the orange zest and return milk to the stovetop over a low heat. Add the chocolate and stir until it has melted, making sure that it doesn't stick to the bottom of the pan.

3 Using an immersion blender fitted with the blending or general purpose blade, whizz for 40 seconds, or until thick and frothy. Pour into four mugs or heatproof glasses and serve hot.

CHOCOLATE LIQUEUR FRAPPE

SERVES 2

260 g (10 oz/2 cups) ice cubes

125 ml (4 fl oz/½ cup) milk

60ml (2 fl oz/¼ cup) cream

2 tablespoons Frangelico or other nut-flavoured liqueur

40 g (1½ oz/⅓ cup) icing (confectioners') sugar

2 tablespoons unsweetened cocoa powder, plus extra, to dust

1 **Put the ice,** milk, cream, Frangelico, icing sugar and cocoa in a blender. Blend until thick and creamy.

2 **Pour into tall glasses,** dust with extra cocoa and serve.

APRICOT EGGNOG

SERVES 4

½ vanilla bean or ½ teaspoon natural vanilla extract

120 g (4¼ oz/⅔ cup) dried apricots

½ cinnamon stick

600 ml (21 fl oz) milk

2 eggs

1½ tablespoons honey

2 teaspoons orange-flavoured liqueur, or to taste

grated nutmeg, to serve

1   **If using the vanilla bean,** split the bean in half and scrape the seeds into a small saucepan. Add the vanilla bean, apricots, cinnamon stick and 150 ml (5 fl oz) of water and bring to the boil over medium heat. Reduce heat and simmer 5 minutes, or until the apricots are soft. Remove from heat and cool slightly.

2   **Discard the vanilla bean,** if using, and cinnamon stick and transfer the mixture to a blender or processor fitted with the metal blade. Whizz for 15–20 seconds, or until smooth.

3   **Add milk,** eggs, honey, liqueur and vanilla extract, if using, and whizz in short bursts until frothy. Divide among four mugs or heatproof glasses and sprinkle with grated nutmeg.

Note: The eggnog can also be chilled, then whizzed briefly until frothy just before serving.

CAFFE LATTE

For the home coffee-making enthusiast with a coffee-making machine. Be your own barista.

1 **This type of coffee** is milkier-tasting than a cappuccino. It is an espresso (also known as a short black in Australia and a single in the United States) that has three times its volume of steam-heated milk.

2 **Pour milk and coffee** simultaneously into a thick glass (or into a cup). In different countries, a latte can have a foam or be served separated into stripes of coffee and milk.

ESPRESSO

For the home coffee-making enthusiast with a coffee-making machine. Be your own barista.

1 An espresso is a single-shot drink that is made from a small quantity of coffee through which water is forced under pressure. This produces a dark, rich coffee topped with an orange-brown crema (foam). The crema should be resilient enough to hold a spoonful of sugar for a couple of seconds. An espresso is also known as a short black in Australia and a single in the United States.

2 Other versions of espresso are caffe corretto and ristretto. The former has been 'corrected' with a shot of alcohol such as grappa, and the latter 'restricted' coffee is an extra-strong espresso made with a little less water.

CAPPUCCINO

For the home coffee-making enthusiast with a coffee-making machine. Be your own barista.

1   **This much-loved type of coffee** is an espresso topped up with milk steamed to silky thickness, the foamy top sometimes receiving a dusting of cocoa powder. Cappuccinos are usually drunk before 11 am in Italy – they are considered too weak and milky to drink after meals or later in the day. And, a true aficionado would never sprinkle the foam with chocolate.

ESPRESSO MACCHIATO

For the home coffee-making enthusiast with a coffee-making machine. Be your own barista.

1 **This is an espresso** 'stained' (which is what macchiato means) with a drop of cold or hot foamed milk. It is usually served in a small cup or glass. Despite being officially a milky coffee, you can get away with drinking this after dinner, even in Italy where milky coffees are generally drunk before 11 am!

CAFFE LATTE FREDDO

For the home coffee-making enthusiast with a coffee-making machine. Be your own barista.

1 **This popular iced coffee** is based on a shot of sweetened espresso and some ice-cold milk. The proportions are one-third espresso to two-thirds milk. The espresso must be hot and the sweetener is dissolved in it. (Sugar does not readily dissolve in a cold liquid.) The hot espresso is poured directly onto the ice-cold milk. Serve the drink with long straws.

2 **Another popular type of iced coffee,** that can also be served as a dessert, is affogato. The term literally means 'poached' or 'drowned'. It refers to a scoop of vanilla ice cream with a shot of liqueur poured over it that is then 'drowned' in a shot of hot espresso.

ORANGE AND CARDAMOM HERBAL TEA

SERVES 2

3 cardamom pods

250 ml (9 fl oz/1 cup) orange juice

3 strips orange zest

2 tablespoons caster (superfine) sugar

1 Place **cardamom pods** on a chopping board and press with the side of a large knife to crack them open. Place the cardamom, orange juice, zest, sugar and 500 ml (17 fl oz/ 2 cups) water in a pan. Stir over medium heat for 10 minutes, or until the sugar has dissolved. Bring to the boil, then remove from the heat.

2 Leave to infuse for 2–3 hours, or until cold.

3 Chill in the refrigerator. Strain and serve over ice.

EARL GREY SUMMER TEA

MAKES 4 X 250 ML GLASSES

1 cinnamon stick

1 tablespoon Earl Grey tea leaves

250 ml (9 fl oz/1 cup) orange juice

2 teaspoons finely grated orange zest

2 tablespoons sugar, to taste

ice cubes

1 orange, sliced into thin rounds

4 cinnamon sticks

1 Place the cinnamon stick, tea leaves, orange juice, orange zest and 750 ml (26 fl oz/3 cups) water in a medium pan.

2 Slowly bring to a simmer over a gentle heat. Once simmering, stir in the sugar, to taste, and stir until dissolved. Remove from the heat and allow to cool.

3 Once the mixture has cooled, strain the liquid into a jug and refrigerate until cold.

4 Serve in a jug with lots of ice cubes, and garnish with the orange slices and extra cinnamon stick.

ORANGE AND GINGER TEA COOLER

SERVES 2

1 small orange

½–1 tablespoon Darjeeling tea leaves

250 ml (9 fl oz/1 cup) ginger beer

8 thin slices glacé ginger

2 tablespoons caster (superfine) sugar

4–6 ice cubes

mint leaves

1 Remove the zest from the orange using a vegetable peeler, avoiding the white pith, and cut into long thin strips. Place half the zest and the tea leaves in a bowl and pour in 500 ml (17 fl oz/2 cups) boiling water. Cover. Leave to steep for 5 minutes, then strain through a fine strainer.

2 Pour into a jug, add ginger beer and chill for 6 hours, or overnight if possible.

3 One hour before serving, add the ginger, sugar and remaining orange zest. Stir well.

4 Pour into tall glasses, add 2–3 ice cubes per glass and garnish with mint leaves.

LEMON GRASS TEA

MAKES 2 X 310 ML GLASSES

3 stalks lemon grass

2 slices lemon

3 teaspoons honey, or to taste

lemon slices

1 **Prepare the lemon grass** by removing the first two tough outer layers. For maximum flavour, only use the bottom one-third of the stalk (the white part). Slice thinly into rings. (You could use the remaining stalks as a garnish, if you like.)

2 **Place the lemon grass in a jug** and cover with 625 ml (22 fl oz/2½ cups) boiling water. Add the lemon slices and cover. Allow to infuse and cool. When cooled to room temperature, strain. Add the honey, to taste. Place the tea in the refrigerator to chill.

3 **To serve,** pour the tea into two glasses with extra slices of lemon. Add ice, if desired.

ICED MINT TEA

SERVES 6

4 peppermint tea bags

115 g (4 oz/⅓ cup) honey

500 ml (17 fl oz/2 cups) grapefruit juice

250 ml (9 fl oz/1 cup) orange juice

mint sprigs

1 Place the tea bags in a large heatproof jug and pour in 750 ml (26 fl oz/3 cups) boiling water. Allow to steep for about 3 minutes, then remove and discard the bags. Stir in honey and allow to cool.

2 Add the grapefruit and orange juice. Cover and chill in the refrigerator. Serve in glasses, garnished with mint.

AMERICAN ICED TEA

MAKES 8 X 250 ML GLASSES

4 Ceylon tea bags

2 tablespoons sugar

2 tablespoons lemon juice

375 ml (13 fl oz/1½ cups) dark grape juice

500 ml (17 fl oz/2 cups) orange juice

375 ml (13 fl oz/1½ cups) ginger ale

ice cubes

lemon slices

1 Place tea bags in a heatproof bowl with 1 litre (34 fl oz/ 4 cups) boiling water. Leave for 3 minutes. Remove the bags and stir in the sugar. Cool.

2 Stir in the juices. Refrigerate until cold, then add the ginger ale. Serve over ice cubes with a slice of lemon.

BASIL, SPEARMINT AND LIQUORICE WAKE-ME-UP

MAKES 2 GLASSES

1 tablespoon liquorice tea leaves

1 tablespoon spearmint tea leaves

10 basil leaves

basil leaves, extra, to serve

1 Put the liquorice and spearmint tea leaves into a teapot. Lightly crush the basil leaves and add them to the pot. Fill the pot with boiling water (about 1 litre/34 fl oz/4 cups), put on the lid and leave to brew for 3 minutes. Strain into teacups and garnish with basil leaves. Serve hot or cold.

Note: As the tea cools, the liquorice flavour becomes stronger and sweeter — add slices of lemon if you find it too strong.

ICED KIWI GREEN TEA

MAKES 4 MEDIUM GLASSES

6 kiwifruit, peeled

1 lemon, thinly sliced

2 green tea bags

2 tablespoons caster (superfine) sugar

ice cubes, to serve

kiwifruit slices, to serve

lemon slices, to serve

1 Juice the kiwifruit through a juice extractor. Put the lemon slices, tea bags and 1.25 litres (44 fl oz/5 cups) boiling water into a heatproof bowl. Set aside to infuse for 5 minutes. Strain and discard the tea bags. Add kiwifruit juice and sugar and stir until sugar has dissolved. Set aside to cool, then chill.

2 Stir to combine and serve over ice, garnished with a slice each of kiwifruit and lemon.

ICED ORANGE AND STRAWBERRY TEA

MAKES 4 MEDIUM GLASSES

3 oranges, peeled

500 g (1 lb 2 oz) strawberries, hulled

2 orange pekoe tea bags

ice cubes, to serve

orange zest, to garnish, optional

1 Juice the oranges and strawberries through a juice extractor. Put the tea bags and 1.25 litres (44 fl oz/5 cups) boiling water in a heatproof bowl. Set aside to infuse for 5 minutes. Discard the tea bags. Stir through the orange and strawberry juice.

2 Chill well. Stir to combine and serve over ice with a twist of orange zest, if desired.

APPLE AND CINNAMON HERBAL TEA

MAKES 2 MEDIUM GLASSES

4 (about 600 g/1lb 8 oz) golden
    delicious apples, roughly chopped

1 cinnamon stick

3–4 tablespoons soft brown sugar

ice cubes, to serve

1 Place the apple, cinnamon stick, brown sugar and 1 litre (4 cups) water in a pan. Bring to the boil, reduce the heat and simmer for 10–15 minutes, or until the flavours have infused and the apples have softened.

2 Remove from the heat, cool slightly, then chill in the refrigerator until cold.

3 When cold, strain and serve over lots of ice.

ICED LEMON AND PEPPERMINT TEA

MAKES 2 MEDIUM GLASSES

2 peppermint tea bags

6 strips lemon zest, about 2 x 5 cm
(1 x 2 inches)

1 tablespoon sugar (or to taste)

ice cubes, to serve

mint leaves, to garnish

1 **Place the tea bags** and lemon zest strips in a large bowl. Cover with 830 ml (28 fl oz/3⅓ cups) boiling water and leave to infuse for 5 minutes.

2 **Squeeze out the tea bags** and discard. Stir in the sugar to taste.

3 **Pour into a jug** and chill. Serve in chilled glasses with ice cubes and mint leaves.

MOROCCAN MINT TEA

1 tablespoon green tea leaves

30 g (1 oz) sugar

1 large handful of spearmint leaves and stalks

1 **Heat the teapot** and add the green tea leaves, sugar and spearmint leaves and stalks. Fill with boiling water and brew for at least 5 minutes. Adjust the sweetness if necessary.

Note: In Morocco, this light sweet tea is often served before, and always after every meal, and is prepared at any hour of the day when friends or guests arrive at a Moroccan home. It is sipped in cafés. Traditionally it is served from a silver teapot into ornately painted glasses.

MOCKTAILS

LIME AND RUBY GRAPEFRUIT SODA

SERVES 4

4 limes

1 ruby grapefruit

350 ml (12 fl oz) lime juice cordial

1 litre (35 fl oz/4 cups) soda water
(club soda), chilled

1 Peel two of the limes using a sharp knife, removing all the white pith. Discard the peel and pith. Cut the peeled limes into segments by cutting between the membranes. Put each lime segment into a hole of an ice-cube tray, cover with water and freeze until firm.

2 Peel the remaining limes and the grapefruit, removing all the white pith. Discard the peel and pith. Put the fruit in a blender or small processor fitted with the metal blade and whizz for 25–45 seconds, or until puréed. Strain into a large pitcher through a coarse sieve; some texture is desirable.

3 Just before serving, add the lime juice cordial and soda water. Pour into four tall glasses and add the lime ice cubes.

Note: The sieved juice can be made up to 24 hours in advance and stored, covered, in the refrigerator.

LEMON, LIME AND SODA WITH CITRUS ICE CUBES

MAKES 2 MEDIUM GLASSES
AND 8 ICE CUBES

1 lime

2½ tablespoons lemon juice

170 ml (6 fl oz/⅔ cup) lime juice cordial

625 ml (22 fl oz/2½ cups) soda water
(club soda), chilled

1 Using a sharp knife, remove the peel and white pith from the lemon and lime. On a chopping board, cut between the membranes to release the segments. Place a lemon and lime segment in each hole of an ice cube tray and cover with water. Freeze for 2–3 hours or overnight until firm.

2 Combine the lemon juice, lime juice cordial and soda water.

3 Pour into long, chilled glasses with the ice cubes.

VIRGIN MARY

SERVES 4

750 ml (27 fl oz/3 cups) tomato juice

2 tablespoons lemon juice

1 tablespoon worcestershire sauce

¼ teaspoon ground nutmeg

few drops Tabasco sauce

1 cup ice (12 ice cubes)

2 lemon slices, halved

1 **Place the tomato juice,** lemon juice, worcestershire sauce, nutmeg and Tabasco sauce in a large pitcher and stir until combined.

2 **Place ice cubes in a blender**; blend for about 30 seconds.

3 **Pour the tomato juice mixture** into serving glasses and add the crushed ice and lemon slices. Season with salt and pepper before serving.

CRANBERRY, RASPBERRY AND VANILLA SLUSHY

MAKES 2 LARGE GLASSES

500 ml (17 fl oz/2 cups) cranberry juice

300 g (11 oz) frozen raspberries

1 tablespoon caster (superfine) sugar

200 g (7 oz) vanilla yoghurt

about 10 ice cubes, crushed

1 Blend the cranberry juice, frozen raspberries, sugar, yoghurt and ice cubes in a blender until smooth.

Note: To make your own vanilla yoghurt, simply scrape the seeds from a vanilla bean into a large tub of natural yoghurt, add the pod and refrigerate overnight.

WATERMELON AND STRAWBERRY SLUSHY

MAKES 6 MEDIUM GLASSES

2 kg (4 lb 8 oz/10 cups) chopped
    watermelon (about 1 large
    watermelon)

250 g (9 oz) strawberries, hulled

2 teaspoons caster (superfine) sugar

1 Combine the watermelon, strawberries and sugar in a bowl. Save some watermelon for garnishing. Blend the mixture in batches in a blender until smooth, then pour into a shallow metal tray. Cover with plastic wrap and freeze for 2–3 hours, or until the mixture begins to freeze.

2 Return to the blender and blend quickly to break up the ice. Pour into 6 glasses, then cut the reserved watermelon into 6 small triangles and fix one onto the edge of each glass.

Note: Think plump and juicy when choosing strawberries to get the best result with this drink.

PINEAPPLE AND LYCHEE CREAMY COLADA

MAKES 6 MEDIUM GLASSES

⅓ pineapple, peeled and chopped

750 ml (27 fl oz/3 cups) pineapple juice

500 g (1 lb 2 oz) tinned lychees and their juice

2 tablespoons spearmint leaves

125 ml (4 fl oz/½ cup) coconut cream

crushed ice

1 Blend the pineapple, pineapple juice, lychees and their juice and spearmint in a blender until smooth. Add coconut cream and crushed ice and blend until thick and smooth.

2 Serve in cocktail glasses with lychees on toothpicks.

Note: For an alcoholic version, add a splash of white rum.

CINDERELLA

SERVES 1

45 ml (1½ fl oz) orange juice

45 ml (1½ fl oz) pineapple juice

15 ml (½ fl oz) lemon juice

ice cubes

1 **Pour the orange juice,** pineapple juice and lemon juice
into a cocktail shaker. Add a scoop of ice, shake vigorously,
then strain into a chilled martini glass.

MIXED BERRY AND PINEAPPLE FRAPPÉ

SERVES 2

200 g (7 oz) fresh or frozen mixed berries

225 g (8 oz/1⅓ cups) chopped pineapple

250 ml (9 oz/1 cup) pineapple juice

½ teaspoon rosewater

6–8 ice cubes, crushed

1 Place the berries, pineapple, pineapple juice, rosewater and ice in a blender and blend until smooth. Pour into two tall chilled glasses.

GRAPE BASH

MAKES 1

10 seedless black grapes

half a small lime, chopped

125 ml (4 oz/½ cup) sparkling grape
   juice

1 Mix the grapes and lime in a tall glass until pulpy, then top
up with the grape juice.

SERVES 6

685 ml (24 fl oz/2¾ cups) lemon juice

310 g (11 oz/1¼ cups) sugar

ice cubes

mint leaves

1 Combine the lemon juice and sugar in a large bowl, stirring until the sugar has dissolved. Pour into a large jug.

2 Add 1.25 litres (44 fl oz/5 cups) water to the jug, stirring well to combine. Chill.

3 To serve, pour over ice cubes. Garnish with mint leaves.

RASPBERRY LEMONADE

SERVES 6

300 g (11 oz) fresh or frozen raspberries, thawed

310 g (11 oz/1¼ cups) caster (superfine) sugar

500 ml (17 fl oz/2 cups) lemon juice

ice cubes

mint leaves

1   **Combine the raspberries** and sugar in a blender and blend until smooth.

2   **Place a strong sieve** over a large bowl and push the mixture through to remove the seeds. Discard the seeds.

3   **Add the lemon juice** and mix well. Pour into a large jug and stir in 1.5 litres (52 fl oz/6 cups) water, then chill.

4   **To serve**, pour over ice cubes. Garnish with mint leaves.

LAVENDER AND ROSE LEMONADE

MAKES 6 SMALL GLASSES

juice and zest of 2 lemons

15 g (½ oz) English lavender flowers, stripped from their stems

110 g (4 oz/1½ cups) sugar

½ teaspoon rosewater

edible pale pink rose petals, to garnish, optional

1 **Put the lemon zest**, lavender flowers, sugar and 500 ml (17 fl oz/2 cups) boiling water into a heatproof jug and mix well. Cover with plastic wrap and set aside for 15 minutes. Strain. Stir through the lemon juice, rosewater and enough cold water to make 1 litre (34 fl oz/4 cups).

2 **Chill well.** Stir to combine and serve garnished with rose petals, if desired.

Note: Add more water, if preferred, for a milder flavour.

MIXED BERRY AND LEMONADE FIZZ

SERVES 4

50 g (2 oz) fresh blueberries

100 g (4 oz) fresh strawberries, hulled

750 ml (26 fl oz/3 cups) lemonade

2 scoops lemon sorbet

1 **Place the berries,** lemonade and lemon sorbet into a blender and purée until well combined.

2 **Pour into chilled glasses** and serve immediately with extra berries, if desired.

Note: Any berries can be used. Use frozen or any fresh berries that are in season.

TROPPOCOCO

SERVES 1

half a small mango, peeled and
    chopped

160 ml (6 fl oz/⅔ cup) pink grapefruit
    juice

60 ml (2 oz/¼ cup) coconut milk

2 teaspoons caster (superfine) sugar

3 large ice cubes

1 **Place the mango,** grapefruit juice, coconut milk, sugar and
ice in a heavy-duty blender and blend until smooth. Pour into
a medium glass.

HAWAIIAN CRUSH

MAKES 2 MEDIUM GLASSES

100 g (4 oz) papaya, peeled, seeded and
  chopped

200 g (7 oz/1 cup) chopped watermelon

250 ml (9 fl oz/1 cup) apple juice

6 large ice cubes

1 Blend the papaya, watermelon, apple juice and ice cubes
in a blender until smooth. Chill well.

BANANA, KIWI AND LEMON FRAPPÉ

MAKES 2 MEDIUM GLASSES

2 bananas, chopped

3 kiwifruit, peeled and chopped

4 scoops lemon sorbet

1 **Blend the banana,** kiwifruit and sorbet in a blender until mixture is smooth.

CINNAMON, MAPLE AND PEAR FRAPPÉ

MAKES 2 LARGE GLASSES

400 g (14 oz) tinned pears in natural juice

½ teaspoon ground cinnamon

1½ tablespoons pure maple syrup

12 large ice cubes

1 **Blend the pears and juice,** maple syrup, cinnamon and ice cubes in a blender until smooth.

Note: Use the best quality maple syrup you can find.

FRESH PINEAPPLE JUICE WITH MANDARIN SORBET

MAKES 2 MEDIUM GLASSES

1 large pineapple, peeled

250 ml (9 fl oz/1 cup) dry ginger ale

4 scoops mandarin sorbet

1 **Juice the pineapple** through a juice extractor. Combine the pineapple juice and dry ginger ale in a large jug and chill. Stir to combine, pour into 2 glasses and top each one with 2 scoops of sorbet.

COCKTAILS

AMARETTO SOUR

SERVES 1

ice cubes

30 ml (1 fl oz) amaretto or other
   almond-flavoured liqueur

30 ml (1 fl oz) lemon juice

30 ml (1 fl oz) orange juice

maraschino cherry, to garnish

1   **Half-fill a cocktail shaker** with ice. Pour in the amaretto, lemon juice and orange juice and shake well.

2   **Strain into a sour glass** (similar to a flute glass, but with a short stem). Garnish with the cherry.

GREAT TASTES DRINKS

SERVES 1

4 lime wedges

10 ml sugar syrup (see Note)

ice cubes

45 ml (1½ fl oz) vodka

mint sprig, to garnish

1 Place lime wedges in a cocktail shaker with the sugar syrup, and squash down with a wooden spoon until limes are fairly well crushed. Fill the shaker one-third full of ice cubes and pour in the vodka.

2 Shake well and strain into an old-fashioned glass half-full of ice. Garnish with the mint.

Note: You can buy sugar syrup ready made. Or, you can easily make your own. See the recipe on page 7.

Variation: Add 8 fresh mint leaves and crush with the limes and sugar syrup.

CAMPARI CRUSH

SERVES 1

crushed ice

30 ml (1 fl oz) gin

30 ml (1 fl oz) Campari

ruby red grapefruit juice

lime wedge

1 **Fill a highball glass** with crushed ice. Add the gin and Campari, then top up with grapefruit juice.

2 **Squeeze a lime wedge** into the glass and add the squeezed wedge to the drink.

SINGAPORE SLING

SERVES 1

ice cubes

45 ml (1½ fl oz) gin

15 ml (½ fl oz) Bénédictine

15 ml (½ fl oz) Cointreau

15 ml (½ fl oz) cherry brandy

30 ml (1 fl oz) orange juice

30 ml (1 fl oz) pineapple juice

dash of lime juice

dash of grenadine

maraschino cherry

1 **Half-fill a cocktail shaker** with ice. Add all the ingredients except for the garnish, then shake well and strain into a tall glass half-filled with ice.

2 **Garnish with** a maraschino cherry.

Note: Created around the eve of World War I, this is the drink that made Singapore's Raffles Hotel famous.

BRANDY ALEXANDER

SERVES 1

ice cubes

30 ml (1 fl oz) brandy

30 ml (1 fl oz) brown crème de cacao

30 ml (1 fl oz) cream

grated nutmeg, to garnish

1 Half-fill a cocktail shaker with ice. Pour in the brandy, crème de cacao and cream, and shake well to combine.

2 Strain into a chilled martini glass and dust with nutmeg grated over two crossed straws.

MALT MAFIA

2 tablespoons raspberries

10 ml (¼ fl oz) sugar syrup (see Note)

ice cubes

45 ml (1½ fl oz) chocolate malt vodka

30 ml (1 fl oz) vanilla liqueur

fresh raspberries, to garnish

1 **Muddle the raspberries** with the sugar syrup in a cocktail shaker. Add a scoop of ice, then the vodka liqueur. Shake vigorously and then strain into a chilled tumbler. Garnish with fresh raspberries.

Note: You can buy sugar syrup ready made. Or, you can easily make your own. See the recipe on page 7.

PERFECT MARTINI

ice cubes

60 ml (2 fl oz) gin

15 ml (½ fl oz) dry vermouth

15 ml (½ fl oz) sweet vermouth

green olives or a lemon twist

1 **Half-fill a mixing glass** with ice. Pour in the gin, dry vermouth and sweet vermouth and stir.

2 **Strain into a chilled martini glass** and garnish with green olives or a twist of lemon.

FLIRTINI

SERVES 1

15 ml (½ fl oz) pineapple vodka

15 ml (½ fl oz) pineapple juice

chilled Champagne or sparkling wine

maraschino cherry

1 **Pour the vodka and pineapple juice** into a chilled martini glass. Slowly top up with Champagne or sparkling wine and garnish with a maraschino cherry.

Note: Many vodka companies are now producing pineapple vodka, but if you can't find it you can use plain vodka.

COSMOPOLITAN

SERVES 1

ice cubes

30 ml (1 fl oz) citrus-flavoured vodka

15 ml (½ fl oz) Cointreau

45 ml (1½ fl oz) cranberry juice

10 ml (¼ fl oz) lime juice

lime twist, to garnish

1 **Half-fill a cocktail shaker** with ice. Pour in the vodka, Cointreau, cranberry juice and lime juice, and shake well.

2 **Strain into a large, chilled martini glass.** Garnish with a twist of lime.

GREAT TASTES DRINKS

GIN FIZZ

ice cubes

45 ml (1½ fl oz) gin

30 ml (1 fl oz) lemon juice

1 teaspoon caster sugar

½ egg white

soda water (club soda), to top up

lemon wedge, to garnish

1 **Half-fill a cocktail shaker** with ice. Pour in the gin, lemon juice, sugar and egg white, then shake well until frothy.

2 **Strain into a highball glass,** half-filled with ice, then top up with soda water. Garnish with a small wedge of lemon.

GIN SLING

SERVES 1

ice cubes

45 ml (1½ fl oz) gin

30 ml (1 fl oz) lemon juice

dash grenadine

10 ml (¼ fl oz) sugar syrup (see Note)

soda water, to top up

1 **Half-fill an old-fashioned glass** with ice. Add the gin, lemon juice, grenadine and sugar syrup, then top up with soda water.

2 **Garnish with** a cocktail umbrella.

Note: You can buy sugar syrup ready made. Or, you can easily make your own. See the recipe on page 7.

HARVEY WALLBANGER

SERVES 1

crushed ice

30 ml (1 fl oz) vodka

30 ml (1 fl oz) Galliano

orange juice, to top up

orange twist, to garnish

1 Half-fill a highball glass with crushed ice. Add the vodka and Galliano, and top up with orange juice.

2 Garnish with a twist of orange.

LONG ISLAND ICED TEA

SERVES 1

ice cubes

15 ml (½ fl oz) white rum

15 ml (½ fl oz) vodka

15 ml (½ fl oz) gin

15 ml (½ fl oz) Cointreau

15 ml (½ fl oz) tequila

½ teaspoon lime juice

cola, to top up

lime wedge, to garnish

1 **Half-fill a highball glass** with ice cubes. Pour in the white rum, vodka, gin, Cointreau, tequila and lime juice, then top up with cola. Stir well with a swizzle stick to combine.

2 **Garnish with** a wedge of lime.

BLACK RUSSIAN

SERVES 1

ice cubes

45 ml (1½ fl oz) vodka

15 ml (½ fl oz) Kahlua, or other coffee-based liqueur

1 Place the ice in an old-fashioned glass, add the vodka and Kahlua, and stir.

CHOCOTINI

SERVES 1

50 g (2 oz) chocolate

ice cubes

60 ml (2 fl oz) vodka

30 ml (1 fl oz) brown crème de cacao

1 **Melt the chocolate** in a heatproof bowl over simmering water. Dip the rim of a martini glass in the chocolate, or dot the chocolate around the rim. Chill the glass.

2 **Half-fill a cocktail shaker** with ice. Add the vodka and crème de cacao, shake vigorously and strain into the chilled martini glass.

MAI TAI

SERVES 1

crushed ice

60 ml (2 fl oz) white rum

30 ml (1 fl oz) dark rum

15 ml (½ fl oz) Cointreau

15 ml (½ fl oz) amaretto, or other
  almond liqueur

15 ml (½ fl oz) lemon juice

90 ml (3 fl oz) pineapple juice

90 ml (3 fl oz) orange juice

15 ml (½ fl oz) sugar syrup (see Note)

dash grenadine

lime slice, to garnish

mint leaves, to garnish

1 **Half-fill a large cocktail glass** with the crushed ice.
Add white rum, dark rum, Cointreau, amaretto, lemon juice,
pineapple juice, orange juice, sugar syrup and grenadine.

2 **Stir and garnish with** a slice of lime and fresh mint leaves.

Note: You can buy sugar syrup ready made. Or, you can easily
make your own. See the recipe on page 7.

MANHATTAN

SERVES 1

ice cubes

60 ml (2 fl oz) whisky

30 ml (1 fl oz) dry vermouth

30 ml (1 fl oz) sweet vermouth

dash of bitters

lemon twist, to garnish

1 **Place a few cubes of ice** into a mixing glass and add the whisky, dry and sweet vermouth, and a dash of bitters. Stir well to combine and then strain into a chilled martini glass.

2 **Garnish with** a twist of lemon.

SCREWDRIVER

SERVES 1

ice cubes

45 ml (1½ fl oz) vodka

orange juice, to top up

orange twist, to garnish

1 Half-fill an old-fashioned glass with ice, pour in the vodka and top up with orange juice.

2 Garnish with a twist of orange.

PINA COLADA

SERVES 1

1 cup crushed ice

45 ml (1½ fl oz) white rum

30 ml (1 fl oz) coconut cream

30 ml (1 fl oz) Malibu

90 ml (3 fl oz) pineapple juice

15 ml (½ fl oz) sugar syrup (see Note)

pineapple leaves, to garnish

1 **Place the ice**, rum, coconut cream, Malibu, pineapple juice and sugar syrup into a blender. Blend well until slushy and pour into a large, chilled cocktail glass.

2 **Garnish with** pineapple leaves.

Note: You can buy sugar syrup ready made. Or, you can easily make your own. See the recipe on page 7.

MOJITO

SERVES 1

2 sprigs of fresh mint

15 ml (½ fl oz) sugar syrup (see Note)

45 ml (1½ fl oz) lime juice

ice cubes

60 ml (2 fl oz) white rum

soda water (club soda), to top up

1 **In a highball glass,** crush the mint and the sugar syrup together with the end of a wooden spoon. Add the lime juice, then three-quarters fill the glass with ice.

2 **Pour in the white rum** and top up with soda water.

Note: You can buy sugar syrup ready made. Or, you can easily make your own. See the recipe on page 7.

PIMM'S PUNCH

SERVES 10

375 ml (13 fl oz/1½ cups) orange juice

ice cubes

400 ml (14 fl oz) Pimm's No. 1

400 ml (14 fl oz) bourbon

185 ml (6 fl oz) sweet vermouth

185 ml (6 fl oz) white rum

1 bottle of Champagne or sparkling
  wine

3 cups chopped fresh fruit (see Note)

thinly sliced cucumber (optional)

mint leaves (optional)

1 **Freeze 90 ml (3 fl oz) of the orange juice** in an ice-cube tray. Half-fill a punch bowl with ice, add the Pimm's, bourbon, vermouth, rum, remaining orange juice and the Champagne or sparkling wine. Stir in the fresh fruit and the frozen orange juice ice cubes. Add cucumber slices and mint leaves, if using.

Note: Strawberries, kiwifruit and slices of orange and lemon can all be used.

BLOODY MARY

SERVES 1

3 ice cubes

45 ml (1½ fl oz) vodka

4 drops of Tabasco sauce

1 teaspoon worcestershire sauce

10 ml (¼ fl oz) lemon juice

pinch of salt

1 grind of black pepper

60 ml (2 fl oz) chilled tomato juice

1 crisp celery stalk

1 Place the ice cubes in a highball glass, pour in the vodka, then add the Tabasco, worcestershire sauce and lemon juice. Add the salt and pepper, then pour in the tomato juice and stir well. Allow to sit for a minute, then garnish with a stalk of celery.

Note: For extra zing, you could garnish your drink with wedges of lemon and lime.

TEQUILA SUNRISE

SERVES 1

ice cubes

30 ml (1 fl oz) tequila

orange juice, to top up

2 dashes grenadine

orange twist, to garnish

1 **Half-fill a highball glass** with ice. Pour in the tequila and top up with orange juice. Add the grenadine by carefully pouring it over the back of a spoon.

2 **Garnish with** a twist of orange.

TOM COLLINS

SERVES 1

ice cubes

60 ml (2 fl oz) gin

60 ml (2 fl oz) lemon juice

15 ml (½ fl oz) sugar syrup (see Note)

soda water (club soda), to top up

stemmed cocktail cherry, to garnish

1 **Half-fill a highball glass** with ice.

2 **Pour in the gin,** lemon juice and sugar syrup. Stir well and top up with soda water.

3 **Garnish with** the cocktail cherry.

Note: You can buy sugar syrup ready made. Or, you can easily make your own. See the recipe on page 7.

WHITE RUSSIAN

SERVES 1

30 ml (1 fl oz) vodka

30 ml (1 fl oz) Kahlua or other coffee-
   flavoured liqueur

ice cubes

60 ml (2 fl oz) milk

1 **Pour the vodka and Kahlua** into an old-fashioned glass half-full of ice.

2 **Float the milk** across the top by carefully pouring it over the back of a teaspoon.

TOBLERONE

SERVES 1

1 teaspoon honey

20 ml (¾ fl oz) chocolate syrup

pinch of finely chopped hazelnuts

ice cubes

30 ml (1 fl oz) Frangelico

15 ml (½ fl oz) Irish cream

15 ml (½ fl oz) Tia Maria

15 ml (½ fl oz) creamy chocolate liqueur

60 ml (2 fl oz) cream

shaved chocolate, to garnish

1 Drizzle the honey and 1 teaspoon chocolate syrup into a large, chilled martini glass, and sprinkle with chopped hazelnuts. Chill.

2 Half-fill a cocktail shaker with ice. Pour in the remaining ingredients, shake well and strain into the prepared martini glass. Garnish with shaved chocolate.

RASPBERRY CHAMPAGNE SPIDER

SERVES 1

1–2 raspberry sorbet balls
chilled Champagne or sparkling wine

1 Place one or two balls of raspberry sorbet in a chilled champagne flute and slowly top up with Champagne or sparkling wine.

Note: Scoop a tub of raspberry sorbet into small balls with a melon baller and freeze until needed.

JAPANESE SLIPPER

SERVES 1

ice cubes

30 ml (1 fl oz) melon liqueur

30 ml (1 fl oz) Cointreau or other orange-flavoured liqueur

15 ml (½ fl oz) lemon juice

maraschino cherry

1 **Half-fill a cocktail shaker** with ice. Add the melon liqueur, Cointreau and lemon juice. Shake well and strain into a chilled cocktail glass.

2 **Garnish with** a maraschino cherry.

INDEX

GREAT TASTES DRINKS